Confessions of a Welfare Mom
Volume 2:
An urban anthology of personal experiences

Kiwan N. Fitch

Confessions of a Welfare Mom:

An Urban Anthology of Personal Experiences

ISBN 13: 978-1-62407-661-9

Copyright © 2013, Kiwan Fitch

All rights reserved. No part of this book may be reproduced in any form, except for the inclusion of brief quotations in a review, without permission in writing from the author or publisher.

Disclaimer: This information in this anthology is solely meant for the purpose of sharing the experiences of the contributors with other readers. The submissions included in this anthology have not been altered to change the meaning and/or experiences of each contributor. The contributor's submissions have not been altered in order for the readers to understand their experiences from the standpoint of the contributors, in their own way and in their own "language." Each contributor has warranted that she is the sole author of her submitted contribution. These confessions are not meant to discredit the Welfare System and/or Department of Social Services. The submissions included do not necessarily reflect the opinion of the Project Author, Kiwan Fitch or the opinion of any of the Kiwan Fitch companies.

Acknowledgements

WOW Volume 2! I have to admit…it wasn't ME. Only GOD could have done this. CWM is not, nor has it ever been, about me. Kiwan is simply good at pulling projects together. It's the women who have shared their truths that give true heart beat to The Confessions Series. Ladies you rock!

I also have to acknowledge that I'm so blessed to have family and friends who have supported me through this process. I just want to say THANK YOU SO MUCH. You will never know how much my boys and I appreciate you and your kindness.

And lastly I would like to acknowledge with a special thank you to FACEBOOK! Social Networking has given me the opportunity to meet so many people who have given this project a life.

CREDITS

Author: Kiwan N. Fitch

Cover Design: Terry Clay Enterprises
www.terriclayinspires.com
tclay2is@yahoo.com

Author Cover Photo: S. Denise Chisolm

Consultants:

Stephanie McKenny
J&J Publishing
www.jjpublishingonline.com

Simone Higgenbothem
ShePheonix Productions
www.shepheonixprod.com
info@shepheonixprod.com

Dedication

This book is dedicated to all the courageous women in my life. I am only able to do what I do because of the support from women who have blessed my life far beyond what I could imagine. There are just too many to name you one by one. So if you are one of the many women who have sowed acts of LOVE in my life... Please know that this book is dedicated to YOU.

Table of Contents

Foreword	9
Introduction	15
Poem by Tina Alexis	19
Lisa Dixon	21
Terri L. Clay	25
LaTeresa Blakely	29
Stephanie Wilson	31
Regina Lewis	33
Mary Hart	37
Iniece Payton	39
Dana Neal	43
Britney Torres	47
Simone O. Higginbotham	49
Christina Stankiewickz	51
Charlsey Sheppard	57
Joe Cheray	69
Sherry Blair	73
Angela Fitch	83
Regina Jenkins	85
Latashia Glover	99
Shalonda Williams	101
Poem by Tina Alexis	105
Poem by Luella Hill-Dudley	107

Contributor Information 109

Bibliography/Resources Guide by Dr. Barbara Milton 113

Foreword

Stacy Rodgers, MSW, ACSW, DVS, WTS

Kiwan N. Fitch is back again with her second installment of the Confessions of a Welfare Mom book series. This follow up book continues with the same theme of narrative reflections of women and their remarkable journeys of navigating through the utilization of government assistance (welfare) in order to improve and sustain the quality of family life and break the cycle of dependency. The contributing authors come from various states, family sizes, experiences. Socio-economic backgrounds, ethnicities, and etc., but despite the differences their remains one commonality: a life free of government assistance. The contributing authors reflect on their lives and their experience being on government assistance and use their story as a source of support and guidance for others.

Despite how they arrived on government assistance and the obstacles placed upon them for utilizing government assistance; these women refused to be just another "welfare mom." The term "welfare mom" refers to women who have children just for the sake of allowing the government to take care of them. However, Ms. Fitch has coined this term into a positive connotation. The term "welfare mom" and its negative implications are not shown in this book series. The stories in the second series continues to depict women who give you the authentic prospective of their personal, sociological, emotional, and familial characteristics that they endured and faced while being recipients of government assistance. Their stories allow readers to see the progress made in the portrayal of government assistance but also demonstrates where flaws still lay.

The issuance of welfare benefits has been controversial throughout U.S. History. If we look back during the colonial period, the welfare policy belief was that the poor were responsive for their own poverty in which they allowed to happen; which in turn lead to the governmental controversy that welfare benefits were seen as a privilege not a right. During the Great Depression of the 1930s, state and local governments began to take some responsibility for providing assistance to the unprivileged. This assistance was working with churches and volunteer agencies to provide the bulk of services that a poor family or individual would need in order to maintain and survive.

The New Deal policies under President Franklin D. Roosevelt included new federal initiatives to help those battling poverty. During the 1930's many individuals were unemployed and the execution of welfare assistance was beyond the financial resources of many states. Nevertheless, the federal government began providing funds directly to individuals or to states for maintaining a standard of living. Between 1935 and 1996, federal programs such as additional welfare benefits, including Medicaid, public housing, food stamps and SSI began to be offered to those who qualified. However; during the 1960's the above additions to welfare benefits were viewed as a "culture of dependency." Supporters of the additional welfare benefits acknowledge despite the flaws in the system such as the financial disincentives associated with taking a low paying job with the risk of losing the array of welfare benefits was concerning to many. However, supporters of the system pointed out that many children are the prime beneficiaries of welfare benefits and removing adults from accessing welfare benefits would have an adverse affect on the children.

During the 1908s and 1990s, disapproval of public welfare increased significantly. Some states required that beneficiaries seek and secure employment within a designated time frame after which welfare benefits would come to a halt. This became known as "workfirst" programs and additions such as job training and child care became vital components of this program. The workfirst programs goal is to reduce welfare costs and move people away from using government dependency for a long period of time.

On August 22, 1996, President Bill Clinton, a Democrat, signed the Personal Responsibility and Work Opportunity Reconciliation Act of 1996 (popularly known as the Welfare Reform Act), a bill passed by the Republican-controlled Congress. The act eliminated welfare programs, placed permanent ceilings on the amount of federal funding for welfare, and gave each state a block grant of money to help run its welfare programs. The law also directs each state legislature to come up with a new welfare plan that meets new federal criteria. Under the 1996 law, federal funds can be used only to provide a total of five years of aid in a lifetime to a family. These and other provisions radically transformed welfare law and welfare programs.

The above welfare history can be seen in the stories shared by many of the contributing authors. The same concerns, criticisms, flaws and positive aspects of the welfare system can be seen now and evident in the stories that you are about to read. The entire concept of this series serves as an empowerment tool for women who are currently on government assistance as well as for the contributing authors serves as an outlet to share their story in hopes of helping another "welfare mom" become redefined.

The "Confessions of a Welfare Mom" series hopes to bring sensitivity and understanding to a complex system that can serve as a means of support or hindrance to those who are seeking assistance. This series also allows readers to not be defined or judged for seeking government assistance, but be viewed as individuals who are faced with some of life's challenges and unforeseen circumstances and require help to get them back on their feet and on the road to independency. This book gives hope to a population that is overlooked and underserved and allows their voices and stories a chance to be heard.

You are now equipped and prepared to take this journey along with our contributing authors. The stories are unedited and are written from a place of truth and empowerment. These authors hope you will be impacted, inspired, educated, and enlighten. I know I was and you will too!

We should measure welfare's success by how many people leave welfare, not by how many are added
~Ronald Regan

Introduction

My name is Kiwan N. Fitch. I am the CEO of The Kiwan N. Fitch, LLC. Which is now renamed The EmPOWERment Corp. LLC. I created my company with a simple mission: to equip "women in transition" with the resources needed for VICTORY! I want them to ACHEIVE success in all areas of their life: mental wellness, physical wellness, education, parenting and economics.

I am proud to present "Confessions of a Welfare Mom Volume 2: An Urban Anthology of Personal Experiences." These women who have shared their personal experiences have taken the stigma and guilt away from the very necessary act. As a nation we are experiencing record numbers of women who are reaching out for assistance, it is a great time to LET YOUR VOICE BE HEARD.

This book series spotlights women who are currently or have at one point in their life time been on any form of public assistance. This includes: TANF (Temporary Assistance for Needy Families), FI (Family Independence), FOOD STAMPS, GENERAL ASSISTANCE, MEDICAID, and OTHER STATE AND COUNTY RUN PROGRAMS. The book is a composite of the many faces of welfare.

As the Co-Founder and Executive Director of a Nonprofit Organization, I created a "welfare to work" program for women who were assigned to our program as a "work site" as a condition of their obtaining benefits. My coordinator and I made sure that our activities were all in line with assuring the full success of the women who we came in contact with. I began this project first as a way to help them see where the cycle of dependency began and identify where, when and how it will end for them.

As the project progressed, I later opened it up to include women who were no longer receiving assistance and are now business owners or career women who are role models for using the systems available to them in order to achieve success in their own rite.

This being my second installment in the Confessions Series, I am just humbled at the response to the project. It has been embraced all across this country. I had no idea what I was embarking on with this undertaking. It is so hard to believe I am currently working on the 3rd Volume. It is my prayer that this project will give readers hope as well as shine light on the subject for those who have very false images of what welfare looks like in America.

I want to also remind you that this project was also designed with a business model in mind. I wanted women who submit to the project to be able to share in the profits. All contributors are affiliates, thus they can make their own profits from sales.

If you are interested in being apart of the Confessions Series we are receiving submissions for future volumes: Confessions of a Teen Mom (Fall 2013), Formerly Incarcerated Mom, Lesbian Mom, Formerly Addicted Mom, and Military Mom.

My prayer is that readers will be enlightened and informed. Enjoy!

Author Tina Alexis

Today We Cry But Tomorrow We Smile

The situations, sorrows and challenges of today do not represent our tomorrows. These situations, sorrows and challenges help to strengthen us to reshape, remold and rebuild our tomorrows.

What you face today does not define who you truly are. These hurts and trials are designed to awaken us to our true selves and to propel us into being who we truly are meant to be. So no matter what we face today, always remember that tomorrow is going to be much greater than what we may be feeling or experiencing today!

We must know and truly believe that <u>The Best Is Yet To Come</u>, and that we are truly worthy and deserving of it! Life's challenges are blessings and miracles in disguise and after the rain a rainbow always follows. Therefore, always remain beautifully blessed and learn to dance and smile in the rain! That is your celebration of the new life that awaits you! Blessings!

Lisa Dixon

Hi world my name is Lisa Dixon, and I'm going to share my story of being a single mom on welfare. In 1998 to 2001 I was on welfare with my daughter and a single mom at the time. I was 32 yrs old pregnant and living with my grandmother, sleeping on her living room floor. One morning my grandmother woke me up with some good old down south breakfast, bacon, eggs, grits, toast with butter or jelly and a big glass of orange juice. At the time I was 4 months pregnant. She sat there and watched me tear that plate up and watch me licking my fingers thinking to myself what she is up to. Little did I know she was fatting me up to tell me I had to get my own apartment before I had the baby because she was too old to hear a baby cry. Now I was already on welfare just getting food stamps, Medicaid and cash assistance. While I was in her house welfare didn't bother me much. So I went to the EAU (emergency assistance unit) that's where you go to start the process of going into a shelter. I went there and stayed there for at least 16 hrs before they placed me into a shelter. Now I stayed in the shelter until my daughter was 4 months old, then moved into my own apartment with my daughter. And that's when the drama started. Once I was in my own apartment, welfare showed me there butts. first thing they did was send me a letter in the mail when my daughter was 6 months old to come in for an appointment to work there WEP program (working experience program) it was mandatory to work WEP or either get your case cut off, rent money, food stamps and Medicaid. They gave me a list of daycare and home providers to watch my child, told me they would pay for it. I had two weeks to find out where and who I was going to have keep my child 9 to 5 Monday thru Friday so that I could work WEP. I had to work them hours because 1. They paid my rent. 2. They gave me food stamps for me and my child. 3. I received Medicaid for me and my child. They also supplied the carfare to get back and forth to WEP. So now here I am taking my 6 months old child to a stranger, work 9 to 5 just to keep my roof over my head and food on the table and medical care. I wouldn't get a paycheck at the end of the week. One day on my pickup day for food stamps and cash assistance, I checked my welfare card and its less then what I usually get like 100 dollars less in food stamps, so now it don't make sense to call cause the phone just rings all day and no one answers. So the next day I go to the welfare office with my child because not only did they cut my money, they stop paying the daycare place. Not thinking to pack food and water to take with me for me and my daughter, I go there and find out they claim I missed an appointment that they sent me in the mail. I told them I never received a letter and their next answer is we'll put it in a fair hearing to see what happen and that takes weeks before you get that. Now they do this to everyone. That's there way of making your life miserable. Now they know you are messing up, so now I gotta keep going to this office everyday to fight for my case instead of waiting weeks for a fair hearing because I need food for the both of us and not only is the food stamps cut, so is the cash assistance. Now at that time I was getting $105.00 every two weeks for me and my daughter in cash, $275 in food stamps a month and $250 rent a month Now with $105.00 every two weeks, I have to pay light and gas, cable, pampers, toilet tissue, and whatever else I needed that food stamps didn't pay for. So imagine $275 a month in food stamps being cut $100 less for a month for two people. And let's not forget about the rent that got cut all together. Now here I am carrying my child with me to welfare office with a bag of pampers, baby food, sandwich for me to eat and please don't let me forget 2 bottles of water to drink because there is no water fountain in the welfare office for anyone to drink. They don't have a play area for the kids so people's kids are all over the place for being there all day. There is no in and out you're there alllllll dayy. So you better bring whatever you need cause if you leave to go to the store that's when your name might be called and you will never know until its time for them to close and they tell you come back tomorrow; just to sit there all day again. Now here in New York, the welfare system sucks big time. That is no place to bring a baby to while you wait for an appointment or trying to get your case back on. That alone is what made me fight for myself to go back to school to get a trade, get a job and get off welfare. Thank You.

Terri L. Clay

Dumping the Check to Live a Life on Purpose

Welfare??? Who me? I thought; no I couldn't be the one in the welfare office. The first time was humiliating and I was embarrassed and I remember thinking, "I hope I wouldn't be seen there." I never thought I would be the one to receive an AFDC check. It was a mere $380 and the food-stamps were about $400 a month for a family of 3. Not enough to live on. Not enough to help my children have the best in life. I couldn't believe that my choices had put me living in the projects and well below poverty level.

You see I was raised in a two parent household, raised in the church, went to private school and really didn't know the meaning of without. So how did I end up here? Hhhhhmmm!!! Choices are a funny thing, one wrong one and history changes and so does your life. My parents forbade me to date my kids' father, but I began sneak and date him behind their backs and eventually became pregnant with my first child. My children's father was working and supportive at first so I hadn't needed to get on welfare. Within a years time I was pregnant with my second child, he was unemployed and I was forced to go and draw a welfare check.

How embarrassed I was. I hated being stuck in that position. You see if I got a job then I would have to pay for daycare. If I stayed on a check then I wouldn't. The check wasn't enough and neither was working a low end job. I knew I had to get out, I could not remain in a life where there wasn't any money by the 3rd or 4th of the month. It was a miserable feeling just sitting and waiting for the check to come. It was miserable being stuck.

Finally I had to make a decision. I MUST get off. That decision came after having 4 children with my crack and alcohol addicted "baby daddy" (as they call it now days) who eventfully dumped me and them for other people. He made the decision to NEVER be a real father to his children. So I had to do something.

I decided to go back to school and get an education. I figured that would be a great way to get off of the system. I had heard that nursing was a great field to get into and without much thought I enrolled into school to become a nurse.

The journey to become a nurse came with a lot of trials of tribulations and test to see if I would endure to the end. I failed many, many classes only to repeat them and pass. I was lied on my instructors and got put out of the nursing program 3 times for various reasons. My children and I had no electricity and water for 3 months. Finally my push, drive and persistence paid off. I finally graduated as a LPN with the intent to return back and get my RN in a few months after graduation.

Once I got a job, I was immediately removed from food-stamps and welfare only to realize that my $12 an hour job just wasn't cutting it. I realized in a few months that I was unhappy at nursing and it really wasn't a fit for me. It was then that I read the book "Purpose Driven Life." That told me that I had been created with a thought in mind. I finally realized why I so unhappy working as a nurse. It wasn't my purpose. So here I was again stuck. Now I was stuck working in a job that I hated. I couldn't go back on welfare, but I also couldn't stay stuck at this job.

It was then that I prayed to God to reveal to me what I was created to do. It was 3 years later when I heard a sermon by T.D Jakes, saying "if you look along the course of your life you will see inklings of your purpose." I started to realize that I had the gift of encouragement. I could speak well and had a passion to help people be better. I realized that my misery at not walking in my purpose would put me on a mission to help people find out what God had created them to do.

Thus, I became a motivational speaker and business owner of Terri Clay Enterprises, a company that provides tools to help people live on purpose and to push towards their destiny. My passion to help others live a life on purpose helped me to host my own radio show called "The Talking with Terri Show." I founded a non-profit, Steppin Out Of The Box, it would help low-income kids to travel and see the world. I became known as the one to help people to push toward their destiny.

When I looked back on my life on welfare, living a life full of days with no money, having no food at times, living in the dark, living in a world of lack the most important lesson learned was, no job or career will fulfill you unless it's what God created you to be. We must all live a life of purpose and be the YOU God intended you to be.

LaTersa Blakely

I must be honest and be real. I have been on food stamps a couple of times in my life and no I'm not ashamed. I first was on them in college. I had my own apartment and as a college student, you were allowed a certain amount. It helped me tremendously and I got off them as soon as I graduated from college and started working full time with the government. Then, back in 2006, when God blessed me with my first child, I was in graduate school at the time, so I too, like any other mother in school, I needed some help; I signed up for WIC, and Medicaid. Yes, I said it, Medicaid and Food Stamps. I'm not going to lie; it helped me out in ways beyond words. Now, if for those of you reading this and you're moms, then you know how expensive formula and baby food can be. So imagine this for a moment, what if it was no such thing as the system, a lot of you including myself would have been up the creek and BROKE. So, again, after graduating from graduate school in 2007, I was still on them. You know why, I was unemployed for the first time since being under aged to work. But, the funny thing about this was, it was not just me I had to take care of, but a little person as well. See I was the type of woman, that was used to going and coming as I pleased, keeping my nieces and nephews when I felt like it or until they worked my last nerve. I had to get back on Medicaid and Food Stamps, and even after I found a job, because of all the hours I would miss due to my baby getting sick or whatever, when his father couldn't take off from work, I had to go. "As I always say, I'm a mother first and if something happens to one of my babies, I have to go, I'll answer questions later. So I would say that for me, I think the program is awesome for women and mothers who are trying to better themselves and not trying to take advantage of the system. When you can do better, then take yourself off the welfare, and leave it for the mothers who are truly struggling.

I was able to buy food for my kids; we were not hungry at any given time, because of the WIC program and the food stamp program. I never had to use the TANF program because my husband, (boyfriend) at the time, always took care of his part. But, I'm speaking from a mother's point of view, I loved going to Wal-Mart and grocery shopping, being able to get my kids some of their favorite snacks. Now, when I go to the store, I have to use the calculator because we are not on food stamps and every penny counts. So to all of the mothers, who are currently on the system, hold your head up and don't be ashamed. You are doing what any other mother would do for yourself and your children. When you can afford to do better, than by all means, do so!!!!!!!!!!!

Stephanie Wilson

What I'm about to tell you is the most private thing in my life. My name is Stephanie and I had to go get on Food stamps to take care of my kids. I worked all my life helping women and kids, but was so embarrassed to go get help myself, my back was against the wall in my first marriage. I thought I married my prince charming, but after the first 5 years shit went downhill. I suffered 10 years of mental, verbal and physical abuse. The verbal abuse was worst then the physical abuse. He always told me I was fat, with two kids and wouldn't be worth shit, but meanwhile I was working at an non-profit place teaching women how not to take the abuse then I would go home at night and was being abused. So one day I got the courage to leave after he broke my ribs and he got caught cheating. I packed up my kids and moved out. So now all the bills are all on me plus my kids were in private schools. So yes, I had to go ask for help. It killed me inside because I was always helping people and I came from a great two-parent home, went to good schools and then to college. I had a full-time and a part-time job and yeah I thought I was the best bitch walking. I didn't need help, I didn't need in public assistance. Growing up I was always told that it was for girls who were having kids after kids and lazy girls who didn't want anything in life. I had to humble myself and go get a case number. I cried for weeks, saying to myself what if people found out. What would be even worse is what if my mother found out, she would kill me. My ex-husband didn't want to help with his kids so I had to take him to court to get the little child support I was getting. Once I went there were some people who take advantage of the system, but then it's others who went on the system to better themselves by going to school learning a trade and then getting off the system. With my story I was laid off from both jobs, collected my unemployment and found my passion in cooking then I started making my own spices, sauces and spreads. My sister then talked to me about starting my own business and attending a small business class. So I started doing small catering events, selling my spices and teaching women how to cook healthy all while I was going through stressful things myself. My sister, Kiwan was the best! She gave me the help I needed to help me get my shit together. She helped name my business which is called, "What's Really Cooking?" I give advice from the stove to the table. My next step is to write a cookbook, calendar and hopefully an advice cooking television show. So in a way I am glad I went to get some help because it really helped me become the entrepreneur that I am today. As far as the rest of my life I am happily remarried with a new daughter. My story will keep getting better as long as I stay true to myself.

Regina Lewis

"Mommy, you said we were going to Columbus! That sign says Cleveland!" Ok.

"Yes, sweetheart, I know." I looked up at the sign and took a deep sigh. The cold pushed my breath even further into the night air. My three boys, ages 5, 4 and 1 at the time, were exhausted after the ten hour bus ride. I was pushing a stroller, trying to juggle our belongings and attempting to figure out our next move. Because of inclement weather, we missed our connection and because it was the middle of the night and there were no other buses going to our destination, we were detoured over 100 miles north.

"Let's go inside for a second," I said. The warmth of the bus station was a stark contrast to the outside cold.

I placed a call to my girlfriend, a reservation specialist at a major hotel chain. She was able to get us a hotel room in Cleveland for the night. I now had my second wind and my despair flew out the window.

"Come on boys. We are going to stay in a hotel tonight and start out tomorrow morning." Luckily, the hotel was a short walk from the bus station. We must have looked a sight walking into the lobby of the downtown hotel but the desk agent was very kind and overlooked our appearance. We were given our room key, wished a good night and we boarded the elevator.

Once in the room, the boys immediately got ready for bed. It was 11:00 p.m. and we had been on the road since 9:00 a.m. I tucked them into the beds and they quickly fell asleep.

The quiet in the room left me to my own thoughts for the first time all day. What in the world was I doing? Was it the right thing for my boys? As I looked at their peaceful faces, I knew anything had to be better than what we had just left.

In 2007, I was a single mom living in an 872 square foot two-bedroom apartment with three rambunctious boys. Every day, I got my kids ready to go to a sitter, boarded a bus to work, put in my work hours and came home. I was barely making enough to make ends meet and food stamps were a huge supplement in the household. Housing in the metropolitan area where we lived was among some of the highest in the country and many people had roommates to cut costs. I was fast approaching my 40th birthday and I was depressed. I was working hard, taking care of my boys and doing the best I could. My life felt like a hamster wheel. There had to be something better for me and my boys.

It was time to stop talking and whining and time to take action. With the help of my sister, I began to research other cities and the possibility of relocating. I narrowed my list down to the Midwest, in large part because of its proximity to my parents. With the help of a realtor in my target city, I found a beautiful home (1500 square feet compared to my box of an apartment). The mortgage was more than half of my rent! All of this was done virtually, sight unseen. I had faith in God that moving was our destiny. I told my family and friends of my plan. Suffice it to say, they were astonished and a few even predicted I would fail. My faith never wavered.

On the day we were scheduled to leave, I said goodbye to those who mattered most and ignored the doubters. It was time to start a new life! The movers would be meeting us in our new city. I had long talks with the boys about the upcoming move. You see, we had never lived outside of our area. We were going to a place where we knew not one soul.

"Mommy, are we going to be okay?" My oldest son asked.
"Yes, baby. We are going to be just fine. Have faith in God."
So, with nothing but hopes and dreams ahead of us, we boarded the bus and shut the door on our old life. Goodbye renter, hello homeowner!

The house I originally bought turned out to have a few expensive issues so we ended up moving again, but within the same state. My workload had exploded and I had more than enough work to make ends meet, working from home. I felt so empowered going to my local social services office and telling them I no longer needed their help. I never let the fact that I was on welfare define me. It was something I had to do. Just another one of life's little road bumps, if you will.

My sons interrupted my thoughts. "Mommy, can we go outside?" In our old apartment, I never would have allowed them to go out without me.

"Sure," I smiled. I opened the door and let them go play in our new yard.

Mary Hart

My story on welfare began when I got pregnant with my daughter. I was married, but my husband and I separated and he didn't offer any support of any kind. Welfare enabled me to stay home with my daughter until she was six years old. When she was six and ready for school, President Jimmie Carter started the WIN program. It offered job training, interviewing skills and dressing for success classes. Mayor Marion Berry embraced the program; he threw open the doors of the District of Columbia. I went to work for the Bureau of Child Support office as a GS clerk. They hired several women who were on welfare; some of them are still there. No one put us down for being on welfare and they supported you. My next stint on welfare lasted less than one year. The state offered job assistance programs. The jobs program is the same as the WIN program. I didn't care, it helped me get and keep the job. I went to work at a law firm. I went from $245 month to $19,000 a year. You have to take advantage of every opportunity and make the most of those opportunities. You have to have faith in your skills and abilities. There will be people who say you can't make it or do it. I say you can. Look deep within yourself and remember if GOD is for who can be against you.

Iniece Payton

Feeling worthless, belittled, defeated and below everyone with a job, yes that's exactly how I felt. I remember the first time I had to go sit in the welfare waiting area to be called.

Remember the AJAX commercial where all the houses were dirty and there was one house stuck out? The saying was "AJAX WAS HERE" LOL. Well that's how I felt sitting there eight months pregnant wearing a summer white dress in the summer time.
Not being able to support my first born took an extreme toll on me and my self-confidence. When we are little girls, we dream of the right man, the wedding, the career and the beautiful family we would have. We never (well most of us) would imagine our children's father becoming a dead beat so and so then leave when times got rough.

I did what I had to do as a woman and a mother would do. Don't get me wrong, he was there until she was 5 years old physically, but not financially and emotionally, it was all ME. If it wasn't for the grace of God and my mother, I don't know what I would have done. Being on welfare not only has its downside like being talked to without respect, being degraded, it has a lot of ups such as training for many job fields, housing, school vouchers, furniture vouchers, and many other attributes. Actually, being on welfare you have access to so much, but you have to ask the right questions because a lot of the workers are not going to tell you.

I was on welfare for quite some time. Once I was hired at the court house I knew I could say bye bye…don't need you no more. BUUUUTTTT, I was laid off 12 years later and guess what…. HELLOOO Welfare. LOL My mother always told me to never say never, I did and again she was right….DAMN!

Not locating a job right away was a bitter pill to swallow and being home all the time drove me crazy. Once I realized that I could take time to finish college and spend more time with my children, I was better than good. I was able to finish up my Associates Degree in Psychology. And now I'm attending New Jersey City University working on my Bachelor's degree. I have 2 part-time jobs! I also am training to be a Gynecological Training Associate. I'm also in a total different state of mind. I also graduated PSI BETA honors.

I can't totally knock welfare because the system wants you to have nothing, but if you do the leg work and the right research you can gain so much from them while keeping food in your home.

Welfare should not be a life choice, but rather a resource to a more independent future. Sometimes in the life we need to take a few steps backward in order to leap forward. And right now IM LEAPING BABY!!! BLESSINGS…

Dana Neal

I was not scared, I was challenged; challenged in trying to use all that I knew to live this new life as a young mom. I was eighteen. I was expecting and I was on welfare. Very different from other young moms, I chose to go on welfare to help me with my unborn child where I couldn't. I was a freshman in college, living at home, and looking at life day to day. I applied for welfare because I needed funds to take care of myself and to get ready for my unborn child. For years, I stayed this way; never abusing the system, just utilizing what I needed to get by. I had three children, obtained various educational certificates and one degree and started working. By the time my oldest was ten years old, I had been on and off of welfare.

When I first applied for government assistance, they, the government, said I can only have $440 a month for my daughter and myself. Living at home, that was fine, but when I decided to move out the rent was $300, lights and gas where $100 and the option to get a phone was not there. At this time having a cell phone was a luxury people like me didn't have. I was allotted enough in food stamps to have food in the house, but I struggled every month with trying to get diapers, or even going to the laundry mat. When I left my mother's home I no longer had the convenience to get to the grocery store, so paying for a cab, well, I shopped at the corner stores, it was a challenge.

I learned quite quickly how to get what I needed; I did what the government asked. I joined a program that would pay for daycare and allow me to go to school, and also give me transportation to and from school. I had two of the greatest case workers ever. They supported me in my endeavors, couldn't understand why I was still on welfare, when I had the mind to do what was needed to get off. They even understood that I had low self-esteem and felt like tomorrow was as far into the future that I could see. I attended Milwaukee Area Technical College starting in 1991 where, after changing my major twice, having a second child, I obtained my Associates Degree in Police Science in December of 1995.

During this time I moved again and started looking at what welfare was doing for me and my family. Every month I had to tell them who lived in my house, and who didn't, who were the fathers of my children and being forced to report those Dads to child support. I was still battling self-esteem issues dating the lowliest of low, being beat-up for no reason and hiding that from my kids. I knew I had anger issues because of what I was holding in, but WOW! If it wasn't the man in my life it was big brother spying on my life. You know what; they had a right to spy on me in a sense. They were giving me a monthly stipend with food stamps, a way to school and daycare for my children. They had the authority to take it all back whenever they wanted to. Do you understand what that means? My life was myself, my children, my government. I was featured on one or two local news shows about my life and how I was making well as a single mom and on welfare. I was a feature to them when I couldn't even feature myself.

After obtaining my associates degree, I got a great job and was soon off of welfare, or so I thought. The job I had ended after six months. It was a grant funded program and the money ran out. After four months on unemployment, I found another low-end job; I found myself re-applying for welfare. Now receiving almost $515 for two kids and a little in food stamps; with the job, I was able to keep bills paid and a roof over our heads. I was driving my own car, in a nice apartment, in a good neighborhood, but back on welfare. The problem here was I was allowing THEM (the government) to get back in my life and in my business. It didn't help that I was expecting my third child.

Although the system allowed me to have $675 for my family, no matter how big or how small, and the food stamps were enough I was starting to feel inadequate, again, as an educated mom not doing enough. I got a job determined to get off of welfare completely, again so I thought. My youngest child was born with health issues; I had to quit my secure 9-5 to work at his daycare and then had to leave there because I needed to be close to him all the time at home.

By this time welfare was W-2(Welfare Works) in Wisconsin. I was at a point where I knew we couldn't live like this forever. We were not going to be a generational family on welfare. I took night classes on starting a business, I went back to a traditional, secure 9-5 and by the time my youngest was two years old, I was completely off of welfare (or W-2).

I'm glad the government benefits were available and they helped me obtain one degree at that time in my life. I am now married with four children (in a blended family), I have a Bachelors Degree in Criminal Justice and I'm in entrepreneur. The children I birthed are 21, 17 and 13 and living a full life. I thank God for the opportunity to share my story. Being on welfare was not a bad thing; I never abused the system, I learned how it could help me if I let it.

Britney Torres

I'm Britney T and I'm 19 years old with two children. I am a single parent. I became a mother on welfare in 2009 when I was placed in an Mommy and Me program. I was placed in this program because my children and I were removed from my parent's house due to problems. I moved in on September 25 2009, two days before my birthday. I started receiving TANF in October. Being in this program I was told to go to school and get a high school diploma. I began going to school in Irvington. I've been going to school for two years and finally graduated in the summer class of 2011. I had my moments when I didn't want to be here or do anything they asked. Being here made me realize that my kids are depending on me to do right and make their lives better. Being here made me mature a whole lot. I never thought I would make it as far as I did. My only income was welfare and the help of my parents helped as well. I really didn't have a bad experience with welfare until now. It's so hard to get in contact with my housing worker. She never picks up or calls back. I do my part, but she doesn't do hers. It's been about two months I've been calling her, but she never responds. It takes my school day to go all the way to New Brunswick now because welfare is no longer located in Amboy. I've only seen my housing worker once when I first went for my TRA. I have been back at least seven times and she never comes out so now she has people coming out that don't even know my case, so nothing is getting done right. Come to think of it, I moved my welfare case from East Orange to Perth Amboy. It's been like that for five months already. I still don't have a welfare worker for TANF. It's like my life is getting better so now things want to go wrong with people. They ask for so much, but never want to get their part done. It's okay though I'm going to get my part done and make sure I do what I have to do to better my life. I graduated high school and got accepted into Lincoln Tech for the medical assistant program and finally moving out. The Mommy and Me program helped me to build a family with my children. Thanks to my parents and Isaiah House staff for helping it come to an end here and starting a new chapter in my life.

Simone O. Higginbotham

If my memory serves me correctly I was a single mother even when I was married to my daughter's father. I can remember the exact moment I became a single mother. One fall morning I had to borrow my now ex-husband's car because mine had temporarily died. On that ride to work I discovered a letter in his car along with a picture. At that very moment I was done with all the cheating, deception, lies and verbal abuse. I continued to work and once I arrived I asked the stockperson to put me some boxes to the side. The day went quickly and I arrived back at home. I entered the house with the boxes and he asked, "What are the boxes for?" I replied, "For you, I am tired of living like this and my daughter seeing it and thinking that this is the way relationships are suppose to be."

That night after I had cooked and fed my child, I settled into the bathtub and I prayed and asked God to help me to be strong and not to allow this man back into my life. After that night I have worked hard at trying to maintain a home for us. It has not been easy, I have had to do things that I have not wanted to do, but I had to provide for my daughter. I have been on Food Stamps; received food from Food Pantry's and even worked jobs where the boss has degraded me. Over the years I have had men in my life that I was involved with because I was able to receive money from them to make ends meet. My daughter's father was ordered to pay $42.00 a month child support and no matter how I stretched it, I was never able to care for her with just that. I had to do what I had to do. I can take solace in that I never did anything illegal to provide for her.

My divorce was final nearly 13 years ago and my daughter recently turned 18 years old. She is a strong, independent and smart young woman. I would like to credit the fact that I was strong enough to become a single mother. It has not been easy, but I never gave up. Last year I became the Co-Owner of a Woman's magazine that was conceived to inspire and empower women just like me. And in December I will receive my B.S. in Business Management. Through it all I have managed to overcome an abusive marriage, bad divorce and life filled with ups and downs. The end result was being able to find out what I was made of and raising a beautiful young woman whom I hope will learn from her mother's mistakes and accomplishments.

Christina Stankiewickz

My name is Christina Alexis Stankiewickz. I was born in 1973 in an Italian neighborhood in North-Eastern Philadelphia. My family consisted of my mom, Anne, an Irish Italian catholic woman, my dad, Paul, an Irish Italian catholic man, my brother Paul who is four years older than me, and my sister Annemarie who is three years older than me I'm the baby. Life was filled with real normal family dinners, Sunday pasta at grandma's house. My brother, and my sister and I never wanted for nothing especially food that was just given. Then in 1979 my mom and my dad split up; my mom moved to New Jersey and life changed. My mom was a manager at a food restaurant, but with three kids to provide for. Now by no means was my father a dead beat dad. He paid support and took us on weekends, but my mother struggled none the less and was forced to go for welfare and received food stamps. Back then they were paper checks. I can still remember my mom sending us kids to the store and giving Paul, the oldest, the stamps. We were in check out line and we really didn't know how it worked so Paul went to pay and the lady held the stamps up and said this is a food stamp order holding up the line. To this day I am mortified from that childhood memory. I told myself I will never be a welfare mom. I would do whatever work, however long that would not be me. So I got my first job at 14 as a shop back girl at Pathmark in our home town, by this time my mother was remarried to Joseph

B., Chief of police in our town. So we weren't struggling anymore which is for some women the only way out of the system; help from partners. For about a year all was good, family dinners, my sister and I were playing cheerleaders for pee wee football, by this time Paul had moved in with my Dad, so it was me and Annemarie again wanted for nothing then a year or a year and a half after my mom and Joe were married they started drinking alcoholism runs in my family. My grandmother was an alcoholic when my mom was coming up. Well the disease took over my parent's life and by that time Annie Marie and I were in high school. We played field hockey and for Annie Marie she excelled in sports. I think she did so she could forget the consequences in our home once again. We had no dinners. God blessed my sister. She got a job at Acme Supermarkets and at the age of 16 or 17 was feeding me, buying me school clothes. The fights between my mom and Joe were violent to the point where I slept with my sister till my Dad came and got us my freshmen year her senior year. Life changed again Annie Marie and I went to a primarily black high school. Our friends were all black; my boyfriend was black and white mix. When we moved we moved to a rich white neighborhood, but no one knew we lived in poverty and that all of us kids shared a bedroom and my Dad slept on the living room floor. GOD blessed my dad and he did the best he could, worked everyday cooked, cleaned, but wouldn't ask my mom or the system for help. So I always felt like I had to hide who I was; with my mom it was hiding the dysfunction of alcoholism in my home, then with Dad that we were dirt poor. By this time I was going to an all white rich school. I was hiding the fact that my boyfriend was black and that in their perfect town was our poor family. I learned at a young age to put on a mask to fit in, and not to air your dirty laundry. What happens at home stays at home. So for my whole life I said I will not be poor when I am old enough to get a job and make money I will work as hard as I can to stay out of the system. My children will never go through what I had to; they will not want for anything and will never go hungry. So when I was in high school my sister and I worked at a pizza place where my dad was a delivery driver for his second job, I worked there until my senior year than worked at Marshalls well I can't tell you all the jobs I had I don't have that much time, the bottom line is I was not afraid to work. I had nice things, moved out when I was with a man so I could have my own, and little did I know I caught the family disease of addiction. When I moved in with this man I worked at the Philadelphia airport, had a nice apartment, nice clothes and had money to go out. Then I had cramps one day and was introduced to Percocet that was the beginning of the end for me. I fell in love I felt like I could work more and do more if I was high so that started my life of using the drugs became more and more stronger and stronger. This lasted on and on until recently. At 24 years old I had a cocaine induced smoke, which left me paralyzed on my left side. I went from a bartender making $300 a night to food stamps and disability. My life was over so I thought I was forced to live with family members because I didn't quality for TANF or most welfare services because I made too much to it, but not enough to LIVE. So I tried to kill myself; by taking a bottle of my prescribed meds. My heart stopped and they revived me. Little did I know that was the first of many times God would save my life.

I will never live on my own, have children. Then I moved on my own again with another family member. Still not getting help from welfare or social security so I tried to die a slow death by using crack/cocaine. Until one day while high I set myself on fire. While in Psychiatric Detox I was introduced to Narcotics Anonymous. I went into a halfway house. Once clean, I left the halfway house to live with my mom's and her boyfriend Joe, because I had nowhere else to go. I stayed clean for one year. Then I had that doom and gloom again because I would never live on my own. When I would go to these agencies to get help they would look at me like I was a looser and spoke nasty to me by telling me that they couldn't help me and they don't understand that the help is life or death for some people. So I used drugs like I always do until I got in trouble with the law and for the first time I was incarcerated. I call my mom my angel who always believed I could get better. She said come to Florida, and I had one week to get into rehab or I had to go. So I did. I went into a great halfway house where I learned I could do the things that I thought I couldn't. I could work and life was not over for me. I got a good part-time job. I still couldn't get assistance with housing, but there was hope. I met the man of my dreams or so I thought. After three years together and being clean and sober I met the first real love of my life Michael A, my 6 pound 8 ounce son.

I thought He would never be exposed to hunger and poverty, and for the early years he wasn't. Until his father lost his job. I went to welfare begging for help with housing and food. And as usual the answer was always the same, "you make too much money." So I did what I used to do best USE drugs. I used and LOST. Lost my son, DYFS (Division of Youth and Family Services) took him when he was 3 years old. I lost my 7 years sobriety. And again I wanted to die. I asked for help and couldn't get it. I was angry and bitter. I used until November 23, 2009, my brother, Paul's birthday. I was arrested. I haven't used since. Today I'm clean and I have my son Michael. Although the struggles haven't changed I have. I completed the program at Isaiah House. We are moving in with a family member because $900 is still not enough to live on our own. I'm going back to school. I'm on my way because God says so.

Charlsey Sheppard

Confession has several different meanings. Confession can be defined as "an admission or acknowledgment that one has done something that one is ashamed or embarrassed about" or as "intimate revelations about a person's private life or occupation." Here I will give my "intimate revelation" about my personal life that I am NOT "ashamed or embarrassed about" *anymore*. To begin my story I feel it is necessary to define a few things such as welfare.

Welfare, like confession, has several meanings and is defined as a "statutory procedure or social effort designed to promote the basic physical and material well-being of people in need." Thereby, social welfare is defined as a "governmental provision of economic assistance to persons in need." These provisions of economic assistance consist of general assistance, healthcare through Medicaid/Medicare, special payments for young mothers and pregnant (also known as Temporary Assistance for Needy Families, TANF) and federal and state housing benefits. I am a single mother who have benefited from ALL of these governmental provisions.

Before I go into details about my life as a "welfare mom" let me tell you about my upbringing. I was born in New York and moved to New Jersey with my mother and siblings at the age of 12. We lived in a nice house on a quiet suburban street in a neighborhood that my mother became very active in; she was a member of the PTO at our schools and later become a member of the Board of Education. I had a decent relationship with my father, whom lived in New York with my paternal family as my maternal family lived in Georgia. I graduated high school in the top 10% of my class with a 4.0 grade point average (GPA) and decided to commute to college upon graduating.

At the age of 19 I decided to drop out of college after completing two years at a four year university. I was "tired" of school. Not only did I drop out of college, I did not withdraw responsibly so now I owe for a semester in which I lost financial aid. In reality, I wasn't tired. I was introduced to a world I knew nothing about; well, I knew about it, I just never lived it. I started hanging out with some friends who I hadn't been around in a while (since graduating high school) and was introduced to a world where test scores, GPAs and deadlines did not exist! This has got to be living! I can stay out all night, spend up all my money and not worry about school... oh yes... this is the life! Then I met a guy. This guy was the COMPLETE opposite of my high school sweetheart that I had just broke up with, who had just received his Bachelor's degree in Computer science, because I was "bored." He was fun and exciting.

Long story short, I began partying more and now I'm drinking and smoking. The only reason *this* life was appealing is because it wasn't structured, it was "cool" and "fun." I wasn't communicating with my mother and father anymore because you know… parents just don't understand. I wasn't hanging out with my little brother and older sister anymore because they weren't cool. I was out having the time of my life chasing a guy that was NO GOOD for me! I was losing friends that just could not bear to see me destroy my life and I did not care because I was having a GOOD time. Slowly but surely I was losing myself and everything I ever learned. Old friends would see me and begin to whisper things like "wow she looks bad" or "what happened to her." I wasn't me!

Then at 20 I got pregnant and said to myself "what am I going to do now?" It was the scariest yet simplest thing that ever happened to me. I remember being so nonchalant about it because I had already had an abortion and grown with my own car and job. Two weeks after finding out I was pregnant, my "boyfriend" was arrested for robbery. Yet, still, I was so nonchalant. I knew I was keeping my baby because abortion was no longer an option. My experience with abortion was horrible and I DID NOT want to go down that road again. The only thing I feared at this point was disappointing my family *AGAIN*!

I lost my job, had already lost my car and now I'm losing my boyfriend. Yet, I was still cool and calm about it. I received unemployment for the first trimester and then it was founded that I was no longer eligible to receive so now I had to think of a back up plan. A few friends of mine were receiving financial assistance through welfare so it was simple, I applied. Shortly after, I began receiving general assistance (GA), cash allowance only, throughout my pregnancy and was eligible to receive Medicaid. My pregnancy was easy besides the trial dates; luckily, my "boyfriend" was home to be with me during my second and third trimester.

I did not report my boyfriend as part of my family because I lived with my mother; therefore I had to file a child support claim against him in which I denied. My family at the time was disappointed at me but they still supported my decisions and helped out as much as possible however, we weren't a wealthy family. Upon delivering a healthy baby girl I decided I had to find myself again and I could no longer have this fun I was having. I was now considered a TANF recipient and not a GA recipient. The change in assistance was due to the fact that I now had a family. With TANF I was eligible for food stamps AND a cash allowance on top of Medicaid for both baby and me. While receiving TANF participants are to adhere to rules and regulations and the one that is strictly enforced is workforce.

Workforce is a program in which TANF recipients attend to receive training in hopes to make you more employable. Through workforce you were allotted a supplemental assistance for childcare. This childcare supplement was only for those participating in workforce or had become employed while on TANF. I attended a workforce class and immediately became frustrated. Here is a program that was suppose to help you become employable by providing training in areas you needed to learn or strengthen or assist you with your job search. I thought I would be able to get assistance with finding a job. NOPE! EVERYONE is put on the SAME level whether you have skills or not! I could not believe it!!! I know how to type, I have a resume, and I have skills in Microsoft office… I DO NOT need training. I needed assistance with finding a job!!! However, I went because I needed the childcare assistance so that I could find a job on my own.

This process was taking another toll on my life. This part of life is NOT fun and is not cool. Where did I go wrong is now the question I am trying to answer. This can't be life! Dealing with social workers talking to you as if you were incompetent or illiterate, dealing with programs that belittled you and not help you, what is going on? What happen to my fun? I can't do welfare because I am not a "welfare" recipient and will not let anyone make me feel less than. Don't these people know I already have self-esteem issues?! How dare they put me in a class with "those" people? I just wanted "temporary assistance." That's it and that's all.

Now during the time I had to apply for GA, TANF and Medicaid I noticed that no matter how you approached these social workers they just did not care about you or your situation. What a shame? I need to have their job! I'd be much better at it. All you have to do is listen and enter information into a system. It can't be that hard, can it? I hated going to the welfare office for anything. If you go late you have a longer wait because EVERYONE is there and if you went early some of the social workers weren't even in the office yet! I'm sitting in this office thinking to myself, Why? Why am I here? I'm looking at the people who are waiting with me and thinking to myself, why are they here? Everyone had a need and the government provided assistance.

How much longer will I need to receive any kind of assistance? I am much better than this. I can make more money than the $322 per month New Jersey welfare provided on top of the $264 in food stamps. This isn't living! I was making twice the $568 at my last job. Ugh! However, I knew I needed the money because the part-time job I had was not enough to buy formula, pampers, shoes and clothes for a baby and take care of my own personal needs. With that said, another rule is to report your earnings once you become employed, in which I did. I was still eligible for childcare assistance and Medicaid. Thank God! However, I was no longer eligible for TANF because my income was too high.

Six months after giving birth I am now a working mother and everything is good. My daughter is in daycare and I do not have to pay for it AND we have health insurance. Then my boyfriend, who was working off and on during the time he was out on bail, was found guilty and sentenced to prison. Another turning point in my life! And this time I am hitting rock bottom! The "love of my life" is gone! What?! How can I live without him? How am I going to raise our daughter alone? Whoa is me! Whoa is me! I shifted quickly into depression; quit my job and lost childcare. I did not care! I sat in my mother's house for months sulking, going to jail visits and accepting collect calls. WOW even as I tell the story I shake my head at myself.

Finally my friends said "snap out of it" and I did! I reapplied for TANF and started all over again! This time I added the fun part of my life back into it. I was partying, drinking and smoking; dealing with the same old thing, workforce and snotty social workers. My "I don't care" attitude was *different*. I REALLY didn't care anymore! I was not going to sit idle any longer. I was going to take back my life whether I did it in the right way or not! I knew how to deal with them [social workers] now. I had figured out that as long as I came early they would respect the fact that I was out of bed before noon; as long as I followed ALL protocols they would respect me enough to listen to my concerns and assist me in the best way possible. The drinking and smoking helped me deal with that.

Then my mother lost her job and that was an indication to me it was time to move out; how selfish of me right? I applied for temporary rental assistance (TRA), a state housing benefit, in order to get my own place. I was working the system now. At this point, I was saying to myself, instead of letting the system break me; I was going to let it make me! I was going to use every resource available to me to get ahead! I wasn't letting social workers talk to me as if I was beneath them. I was citing my rights as a recipient and taking control of my life. Upon being approved for TRA by a retiring social worker, in which I believe helped as many people as she could before retiring, for only reasons she knows, I had found a job with a staffing agency.

I now have my own apartment, a good paying job, TRA, food stamps, Medicaid and childcare assistance. How was I able to obtain all of these at once? I worked the system! Am I saying I cheated the system? No! I took advantage of everything I could! Once I had that mindset there was no stopping me. I had even enrolled back in school at the age of 23, starting from the beginning! I was a single mother. I had to make it to the finish line.

Another turning point in my life came when my best friend died at the age of 25. She was my backbone and it hurt! I had lost my apartment because of failed communication between me and my new social worker for TRA and now I was without a home. My family had relocated down South during all this time so I had no home to return to. I refused to go back to where I had just come from. I had found my purpose in life and decided from there that I would help people realize the value of whom they are in order to succeed in life. I was on a mission, but the only way I knew how to succeed at that point was to continue to look at the glass as half full and live life to the fullest!

After a few hard months I was back in the welfare office. I now only had childcare through a community based program, Medicaid, no job, no food stamps and was barely passing classes. I went to welfare to apply for TANF! The social worker I got this time said to me "everyone here thinks you should be so much further than you are" and with that said I knew that I had to make a change. I didn't realize that I did make an impact on my social workers at that point, something I will learn later. The social worker I had gave me a voucher to assist with my deposit on a new apartment; she gave me food stamps and told me to get a job! And by the grace of God I did! I found another great paying job, in which I was able to afford the rent, and keep up bad habits like partying, drinking and smoking. Again, those bad habits helped me cope.

My bad habits are what crept up on me and began to destroy me. I was spending more than saving; shopping more than paying bills and eventually I lost it all *again*! So what does that say about me!? I was doing the same things and getting the same results! I realized that the only reason I failed is because I let my *infirmity* become my destiny. I wasn't listening to myself, yet alone others. I had people telling me to reach further (social workers, family and good friends) yet; I was looking at it as if they were keeping me down or leading me astray. I was encouraging others to go back to school and find their purpose, yet I was ignoring my own advice (and slightly still do)!

Finally I decided to move down South to be closer to family and break those bad habits. Actually, the change was kind of forced on me; call it will if you may! Now I am 27, receiving food stamp benefits, going to school and starting my own business, Creating Confidence. Creating Confidence is my way of telling people to stop standing in their own way! Recognize their worth and take heed to their own advice. Listen! Learn! Continue to move forward! Never let your setbacks define you or you will lose yourself.

I believe I lost myself as a welfare mother! I was so busy trying hard to prove I wasn't a "welfare mom" and that I was not illiterate or incapable of anything; that I wasn't really doing anything at all!

My advice to other young mothers, single or within family, there is nothing wrong with seeking assistance from programs such as TANF and GA. These programs are designed to help those in need however, be mindful of the fact that it's temporary. READ your rights as a recipient; know what services you qualify for and use them to your advantage. *Don't worry about what others think of you, only worry about the thing you can control and that's your own thoughts of yourself.* Worrying only brings pain and we are all taught to let go and let God! Believe in you!

Joe Cheray

Before I talk about this, let me introduce myself to you. My name is Joe Cheray and I am, as my Twitter profile states, a single mom to a son with cerebral palsy. I live in the heartland of America in Topeka, Kansas. I also have four cats Sunshine, Gracie, Princess, and Dot.

I was born in 1972 to a small town auto mechanic who was also a Korean War vet and a stay at home mom. At the age of 3 my life changed drastically forever. My parents were declared unfit due to my mother's neglect of us, and my three brothers and I were removed from the home. The same night my brothers and I were removed from the home my dad killed himself. Two days later we went to his funeral and then we had to return to our foster parents.

We would then spend the next two years roughly in foster homes in various small Kansas towns. We were separated, two of us went to one town, and my baby brother and I were in a foster home together in Frankfort briefly then separated. I would also spend time on a small farm in north east Kansas.

At the age of 5 we were reunited with our grandparents and our mom in small unincorporated Baileyville, Kansas. At the age of 6 my mom decided that my grandparents had things under control in the raising of us and ditched us. We were abandoned by her and left for our grandparents to raise us.

At the age of 10 my grandfather who was physically abusing me, began to also sexually abuse me. Physical abuse included, but was not limited to being whipped with a bullwhip, getting thrown around my room like a rag doll, and once I was beat until I almost urinated on myself. Throw into that mix the emotional abuse. The sexual abuse started as fondling and moved into oral sex. He had already been physically abusing me between the ages of 7 and 10.

During this time I attempted suicide twice and tried to run away a couple of times. Running away never worked my grandfather controlled the whole county.

The last straw was at the age of 15 when I discovered my pubescent brothers had been going into my room and I vehemently stated that no one was allowed in my room. My grandfather went off and called me a bitch, a whore, and a slut and told me he could go into my room any time he felt like it. He ransacked my room; tearing my curtains off my windows, turning my bed upside down and taking all of my drawers out of my dresser then dumping my clothes out. After I was done hanging up my laundry I had to go clean up my room.

After he had fallen asleep after Sunday dinner I lied to my grandmother and told her I was going to bike the back roads. Instead I biked to a nearby town of Seneca and found my high school counselor. I told her that I was not going back home and that I would kill myself or her before going back home. I would spend the next 6 months in a foster home. In July of that year I went to live with my mom who I thought had her act together and was living in Topeka, Kansas.

I wish I could say life was happily ever after getting out of the hell on earth I was living in, but with it brought future relationship issues and challenges.

I ended up in and out of temporary living situations, being homeless for a bit, and going back into a foster home. I had already found my first abuser. I was also 3 months pregnant when I graduated from high school. I gave the baby up for adoption. I would later go on to be in 3 abusive dysfunctional relationships. The second one brought me the one major joy in my life-my son. I vowed to keep him and break the cycle of abuse.

The important thing is that I have survived just about everything there is to survive in my life. I don't have chapters, I have books it seems. What I have just told you in regards to my grandfather is just a sample of what I went through.

My grandfather has been gone for 2 years. I cried tears of relief and joy at his funeral. I was relieved that I was able to speak my mind to him during his last days of semi lucidity. I was joyous that I was finally free of his physical presence here on earth.

Sherry Blair

Positivity, Gratitude & Greatness

What you focus on expands, and when you focus on the goodness in your life, you create more of it. Opportunities, relationships, even money flowed my way when I learned to be grateful no matter what happened in my life. - Oprah Winfrey

Honesty

The notion of writing this story was a bit of a challenge for me because I inherently have a gift for staying focused on the positive things in life and leaving behind the memories of the obstacles I faced. I suppose that is why my work in positive psychology is so meaningful to me because it is who I am. I had to go on welfare once. I think I may have been the only person in my entire family who ever went on public assistance. Indeed, I do not think any of them even knew that for a short while I was a welfare mom. Honestly, to this day, I doubt my son even knows and he is 25 now.

Humility

For me it was shameful and embarrassing to use food stamps. Back in the day, they did not have a food stamp card. You had food stamps and people behind you could see you counting them out. Being on welfare was a lesson in humility because although my grandparents went from poor to working class, we were always expected to work and work hard. Not being able to work right after the birth of my son in 1986 tore at the fiber of my being. Not working and not providing for my family was never an option. Sometimes one can hear me say "I have been hustlin' a buck" since my childhood years. I had to accept the help that allowed me temporary assistance to get back on my feet and in accepting that help, I had to let go of my pride. I remember I shared some of these feelings with my older brother Eddie, and he reminded me that I had been working and paying into these funds for the last decade. I was only 24 then and already had nine years "on the books."

Choices

I made a choice to have my son as a single mother and I needed to do whatever it took to provide for him. I also had taken in my younger brother who was about 18 at the time because my mother put him out of her apartment. I remember the visit to my apartment and having to show that I would keep my food separate from my brother's food because I was not allowed to feed another adult. I offered my brother a shared room with my son and in turn he had to purchase his own food with the child support money my Dad had been giving to my mother. That was also shameful to have someone come in and look in your cabinets and refrigerator. If I felt degraded in the supermarket, this visit sealed the deal. I made a choice not to dwell on those unhealthy negative feelings and vowed that one day I would turn my life around. I did not let go of the dream I had to pursue a college education. Through my tears of shame, I could still hold on to my vision.

Resilient & Resourceful

Eventually I was able to get back to work pretty quickly in the restaurant business and finding babysitters was always a challenge because I worked at night. Additionally, in that business it is challenging to get benefits and I needed healthcare insurance for my child. At that time there was no such thing as family care unless you were on public assistance. I began working and stayed on public assistance because the jobs I found did not pay you "on the books." If the night was slow, or if you were sick or if the weather was bad, you did not make any money. After a while I became paranoid about getting caught and eventually just took myself off the program. I felt it was wrong and therefore I was compromising my integrity and personal code of ethics. Reflecting back I realized how resilient and resourceful I had become. I realized that I could stretch the little money and food I had very far.

Gratitude

I was grateful that I had help for a little while. It helped me to get back on my feet as I slowly was able to find more work and the babysitting that was required to allow me to work. I ended up paying out of pocket for doctors' visits and for my son's inhalers because he had asthma. I also had a friend that worked in the pediatrician's office and they offered me samples to help offset my out-of-pocket expenses. It was a blessing to have that assistance. People need resources like this to exist and without health insurance it is challenging. Learning to be grateful for the blessings in life showed me the true lesson between needing and wanting.

Relating

I tell my story sometimes—about not being the "right kind of white" too. I remember pulling out that welfare card when I ran an addiction group in the Paterson, New Jersey area and the participants saw me as someone who never struggled. I was the director of the program and held my first masters' degree at that time. There was a racial difference as well as most of the participants were African American, Hispanic and Latino. I stopped the group and went to my office to get the welfare card and I held it up. I told them I have been paying my dues and work (even to this day) seven days a week. That changed the energy in the room with the use of appropriate self-disclosure. The "right kind of white" does not go on welfare. By revealing that truth to them however, it helped us relate better. A few of the women came up to me later and stated they could not believe I had ever been on welfare and they thanked me for being "real" with them.

Sharing Greatness

Even though a commonality was shared between myself and the women in that group, I do know, honor and respect the fact I did not face the same challenges that a woman of color faces, and I acknowledge that as a white woman there are certain privileges that were afforded me back then and still to this day. I keep the card in my wallet to this day because that card reminds me of the inner strength I had back then, but did not know it as I know it today. Today I work to stand in my greatness and know that does not mean I lack humility or am not humble. It means I have learned how to love myself in a way that I did not back then. It means by doing so, I can make more of a difference in this world which is my passion. It also means that I can share and spread greatness from deep within my heart and soul.

USA: Unconditional Self-Acceptance

My studies in women's issues shed light that desirable whites had blond hair and blue eyes and were of a higher socio-economic status, educated and polished. Life taught me about not being the right kind of a white as it did my grandmother who came here as an indentured servant and was told because she had a Scottish brogue, she needed to learn how to speak "proper" English. If there were ever a time I knew I would not be the right kind of white, this was my moment to shine that all over the place. Combined with not having gone to college right out of high school, serving people as a waitress or bartender, having a child out of wedlock and then going on welfare, I blew that chance. Social psychology proves this in research, but I did not need to read about it because I lived it. I know how people "accepted" me as an unwed pregnant woman even in my own circle of friends and family and for the most part, none of them were the right kind of whites either. They, however, were a hell of a lot closer to becoming it than I was. They were also not on welfare, single and pregnant. In a way, I brought it on myself by the choice I made to have my son and not to marry. I broke the rules and I had to deal with the social consequences of that decision. More importantly, I had to learn how to accept myself unconditionally and for me that is when the journey toward unconditional self-acceptance began.

Live, Learn & Change: Creating New Cycles

I feel strongly that at times women contribute to their own economic oppression by the choices we make. I remember watching the women in my family being dependent on a man and knew that I did not want to follow that path. Because my son's father who was nine years older than me at the time was not being responsible, I made a choice not to marry him. The message to have a strong work ethic permeated my fiber and because of that I would do whatever it would take to include scrubbing other people's toilets. I did housecleaning for a short while because I was able to bring my son with me as a baby if I needed to and that made it a viable option. It was a means to an end and I had to take those steps. This too was another lesson of humility for me. Today because I work so much I have someone come and clean my apartment and I truly have so much respect for the work they do and I clean before they come. I also admire the women that do this work because some of these women are entrepreneurial and are raising their own children. This work allows the flexibility you require to wear the many hats that women wear. Making a conscious choice to keep the positive things I learned and lived helped me transform and change things for my life. Being taught a strong work ethic was a great lesson and letting go of co-dependency, dependency and unhealthy relationships liberated me. I felt grounded in the fact that I was creating a new cycle in my family system.

Affecting others with Positivity

Because of my experience and the ability to relate it empowered me to affect others with positivity even in someone's darkest moments. I worked once with a woman in a domestic violence transitional housing program for South Asian women. This woman spoke Hindi and Burmese and barely a stitch of English. I spoke not a stitch of the former languages. We sat near a river edge. She was sad, traumatized and ashamed of living in this housing program. I spoke to her through my heart, with my eyes and demonstrated to her that she was taking steps . . . one at a time toward her new life. I used rocks and showed her where she was, where she came from and where she was going. I pointed to the water that was flowing and for her there were troubled waters at that time. She, just like the river continues to flow and just like the rocks on the river's edge, she was creating the change she needed to become in order to love herself enough to complete the program and accept the help in order to change her life. She hugged me and with heart tears in my eyes I knew we communicated in a more powerful way that no words could convey.

My message to you now is to find a way to spread the affects of your positivity. Acts of kindness. Acts of gratefulness. Acts of charity. Do it for yourself and others! It does not matter where you are in your journey of transformation and truth, you can spread positivity and greatness at any time and any moment of your life. Love yourself along the way and accept yourself unconditionally every step of the way.

Pearls of Positivity
Today I continue to find pearls of positivity in my life at home, work and play and I encourage you to do the same. Dig deep down and find and rely on your strengths, values and virtues. Learn ways to make change in your life. Remember it is a process. Sometimes it takes baby steps—one step at a time. There are many ways to do

this and they do not cost a penny. Build your inner wealth and build it in those around you.

I leave you with one last story to hold within your heart: The Two Wolves Within Us

There's an old Cherokee teaching story where an elder tells his grandson, "Within all people, a battle goes on between two wolves. One is negativity—anger, sadness, stress, contempt, disgust, fear, embarrassment, guilt, shame, and hate. The other is positivity: joy, gratitude, serenity, interest, hope, pride, amusement, inspiration, awe, and—above all—love." The grandson asks, "Which wolf wins?" and the old Cherokee replies, "The one you feed."

Be the change you want to see in others and know that your river is flowing and changing creating a new path of greatness and positivity.

Angela Fitch

January 19, 2012 is my father's 25th Birthday Anniversary in Heaven. I write this to honor him. James H. Fitch was a good father.

I was a "welfare Mom" for probably the first five years of both my sons' lives respectively. That's it. Recertifying, collecting data about money that did not exist and feeling like the case manager had my check in her pocket was too much for me; so I decided I would find a way to not be a "welfare slave." I educated myself quickly, determined to make my own way in this world. I stopped doing things that would slow me down. I stopped ignoring my own welfare in favor of "being in the group, with the crowd." I went to school, worked hard and respected the idea of "success."

To this day, success always matters to me and I do not make tons of money. I do take care of myself. I have never been evicted. I have never been more than two weeks behind in my rent. I have maintained my own apartment since the early eighties and I hate not having gas money. It happens.

I will tell a person in a minute, "Please learn to do something with your own hands, so you will be able to take care of yourself in a crunch." I am a Certified Computer Service Technician, a

Seamstress, a driver; an excellent administrative assistant and a good woman in my own right, yeah, my right. I do not have a husband (still looking) but I have good and not so good, men in my life as I need, when I need. I am not perfect by any means; and I have suffered some serious hurts, but I know that every day when I wake up; I am still my own woman!

Submitted by Angela Fitch, 53, Proud Aries, Christian – God Bless all the women of the world!

Regina Jenkins

This is my confession. As for my story, I never dreamed that my life would have turned out the way it did for me. When I was a young girl I did see some family members using the system to help support their families and it was the women, the single mothers raising their young ones and if it was the males in my family, you never knew it. They kept it on the hush, hush.

My dad was a devoted father that did all he had to support his family. My dad would work 2-3 jobs and never wanted to accept help from the government, but I do recall a time or two when I was about 10-11 years old when I had to go to the grocery store to buy a few grocery items and at the time the food stamps were in the funny paper form and back in the early 70's living in Harlem, N.Y. I felt a little embarrassed to use the food stamps coupons. I can remember waiting in the line for a long time just to wait until nobody was on the line to use them and from that moment a sense of fear crept up on me concerning being different. From this day I didn't know where my father received those food stamps coupons, but it never crossed my mind until now.

And times were hard during my upbringing that we had the privilege of using and eating government foods; the big block of cheese that was so good and cheesy; the thick chewy peanut butter that would glue your mouth together and felt so thick going down, it was hard to digest. I remember the WIC that we had to use for the milk, juice, baby food, cereal, eggs and the cereal that nobody really liked at that time, but never thought about it or ever using the system until I became an adult and was not able to work due to the previous miscarriages I had so my pregnancy was probably considered high risk. I decided not to work anymore until I delivered a healthy baby. I was with a man that did get up and work every day, but he was abusing me and was not taking care of the needs that I had to help me through this pregnancy. So while living in sin with him things were changing for me. So back in 1987 or 1988 I went to the welfare system for help for myself and for the living soul that was living inside of me.

When I applied for help, of course they ask you for the whereabouts of the father, and like everybody else, I lied about the father's whereabouts and at that time I was living with the father. Why, because I was in fear that I was not going to get the help if I disclosed his information and also I thought if I were to be honest then welfare was going to contact him and make him pay and that would cause more stress and drama to a hopeless unstable environment, so I lied! Yes I lied to try to get what I needed at that time to help me and my baby.

So I was set up with the usual money, food stamp, Medicaid, and WIC checks so it was okay for a while. Then things were getting worst and worst with my living condition and I needed to leave him because I started to have vision of me hurting him badly and it was causing me to act out of character and I finally left him and moved in with a friend that I had met in school a few years prior to me leaving and we would keep in touch a lot. She would tell me what she went through with her man, her children's father and then I would share with her what I was dealing with. So I left and moved in with her me and my daughter.

I stayed there for a little while then I had to regroup still living on the system, but was feeling bad cuz I needed a place. I couldn't stay at my family cuz it didn't want my daughter's father to locate me and try to convince me to come back home with him. Home with him was not good, but our apartment was big and I love the apartment, but I had to move on. I had to search for a job and apartment, which I did then through the welfare system, got set up with family day care. At the time I had an Aunt that was employed with the family day care system and she knew someone closer to my baby's daddy, but I was so desperate. The rent was affordable and I was close to my homecare provider and she loved my daughter and I felt comfortable with her.

So my life was changing for the better then keeping things honest giving welfare my work hour's proof of income and where I worked. I was not entitled to receive help after a few weeks of working. They cut me off the system. No food stamps, no money, and had to pay a little for childcare and keep the Medicaid.. So trying to stay afloat and feeling good about being independent and began living above what I was able to afford, not living on a budget. I wanted my daughter to have the best of everything. She did have everything a little girl needed, all kinds of toys, clothes, Nike sneakers. She was set, I was set. At least I deceived myself to believe that.

Didn't set a budget and didn't live by one. I started spending money in Lazrus Kid Clothing stores on 125th street and Young World on Fordham Road in the Bronx. Shoes and stuff for me, food and things were not looking good. Trying to figure out a way to still keep my lifestyle and keep my money to myself without paying my rent and other necessary bills. Still looking good and feeling sexy, I was attracting the wrong kind of men and then the most disturbing thing happen. I was attracted to a drug dealer that lived across the street from my baby's home care provider. I would see him more and more and then he asked me to be his girl then I thought my problems would be over. I accepted it then and I started to have sex with him because he told me he would help take care of me and get me the things I needed and give me money and at least I thought I would have anything I needed. Well that was a big lie. I was used for sex and never received a dime. He would come over my house when my daughter wasn't home I didn't play that in front of my child, eat my food, sleep in my bed and never gave me a dime. Feeling that didn't last for too long after me going over his house sleeping with him when he was living with his mom I got tired of this. Then I found myself in another relationship with a second drug dealer, a little younger and the same thing. Well I was behind in my rent and did all I can to keep things together and went back to the welfare for help after one year of being off the system so I took all my check stubs and when I sat in front of the lady that particular day she told me that I was over by a couple of dollars for the requirement to accept any food stamps that I was needing help for. I walked away feeling lost and didn't know what to do. I was behind in my bills and all I had to do is stop my foolish spending, but couldn't see it and things was not good.

I tried to get help from my daughter's father, but it was always a fight going back and forth to court was not an option for me and at the time he was in worst shape then I was and I felt sorry for him and did not pursue support. Out of respect for my daughter I didn't want to put more on her father so I did the best I could do until I met a man in 1991. In this chapter of my life I met my husband, we got married, but things in my life changed and became even more of a struggle I was married and still dealing with more issues than I came in with.

When I met my husband I was working at a full time job and living on my own making a mess in paying bills on time and not having any help from the welfare system. The only thing that I had was the Medicaid and reduced price for the child daycare.
I was feeling very good about myself to a degree because this was my first apartment without living with someone. It was just me and my daughter and it felt real good for a while. Then the loneliness set in more and more and I didn't like it much.

Trying to do all I can do not to go back to the welfare system by looking the part of an independent single woman, but I was sinking fast because of uncontrollable spending habits. It was not long that I lost my first apartment in the Bronx because of not paying my rent on time and owing too much. I was evicted from my apartment and had to move in with a friend across the street until I figured out my next move.

Because of my man and his issues, which I believed help bring me to the position of me losing my apartment I was faced with a hard decision because of his issues of drug abuse and his other issues. I had to make a decision to go live with my family in Jersey City, NJ for a little while, then my second apartment. I thought I would start fresh and make better decisions. I loved my apartment and was still taking care of the bills. I know this apartment was a lot to handle because I was only making a small amount, didn't make a budget and stick to it and I didn't be firm with my man I was now living with in sin with my daughter to get a job and help. He helped me out in other ways I thought was sufficient for that time. He helped me with my daughter by making her breakfast and taking her to school and picking her up for me and at times would have dinner ready for me when I would get home from work. It worked out fine until more problems arose where money was an issue I needed more and his drug habits and his whereabouts became worst and worst and with all the evidence and signs before my face. I still married him and before 6 months within the marriage thingswere at its worst and I had to move away to go and live with my mom. After quitting my job because of the shame of a second black eye, I started working for an organization that helps women and victims of domestic violence and criminal issues.

I stayed with my mom for only a short time until I realized it was time for me to go back to my father's house. My husband was already emotionally and physically involved with a woman 6 months after we married. He left me alone and didn't come to see about me or my daughter nor did he help me to move our things out of the apartment. I was on my way back to South Carolina, a place I didn't like. I had to come up with a plan and I didn't want to get welfare so I found a job working for a convenient store on the graveyard shift. I didn't like the hours, but I took it because I had a plan to work and save money to get my own place so my husband and I could live together. I accepted him back after months of talking on the phone, making peace and moved into my third apartment still with no assistance from welfare. The only thing was the WIC I received and the Medicaid for my daughter to receive medical care.

My husband moved down to South Carolina and lived with me in my third apartment. It was nice, but things went wrong. I took him to work with me because he didn't want me to work the graveyard shift by myself for my safety and within a month's time, I lost my job because of the cameras showed along with people's complaints of my husband's behavior and him eating and drinking without paying and I was fired from my job.

So I was upset and didn't know what to do and found out I was pregnant with twins and there was no option, but to apply for assistance from the welfare from South Carolina, which was approved and started to receive cash a small amount and food stamps.

Well, my husband told me and everyone he wanted to take care of me now that I was carrying twins because twins run in his family his father was an identical twin. I have twins in my family we were both very happy. I got set up with the WIC and everything thinking life was going to finally get better, but was approaching a head on collision. My husband found work, but it was not the type of work he was used to. He found a job working fixing the Highway 52 in St. Stephen, SC. And he had to work in 80-100 weather outdoor rebuilding the highway and always complained about how he hated that job. He started to hang out with a friend that I knew and they began doing drugs more and more and he started to be less and less at home and found out that he had been communicating with the woman he started to see six months after we married and the reason why he came to South Carolina was because he did really miss me and wanted a change of environment and that he was hurt by her decision to get an abortion. And no sooner than that was exposed he left me once again 4 months pregnant with twins and not knowing how I was going to make it so I had to find a way to gain strength. It was about 2-4 weeks I was rushed to the hospital because I was hemorrhaging and was in the process of having a miscarriage due to the stress of my marriage and my husband leaving me pregnant to go to be with another woman. I had dilated to 4-6 centimeters and the contractions were coming and I needed a miracle and God was merciful and it was there I started my prayer life and God allowed the contractions to stop and the dilation stopped and I was in the hospital 4 about 2 months on my back to try to have healthy babies.

My twins came at 34 weeks and they were healthy baby girls, Jaleesa & Khadijah; they were a little underweight, but healthy because that was my prayer. I wanted healthy babies and not to have tubes or wires and their lungs to be mature all their fingers and toes and no birth defects. God did it they were born on a Friday evening on Sept 2, 1994 in Riper Medical Hospital in Moncks Corner, SC. Jaleesa (baby A) was born normal, but Khadijah (baby B) was born foot first, but had no complications, but low sugar and came home within a weeks time even with their low birth weight.

No one helped me out and I had no support from family. The only one that helped me was my oldest daughter, Shaday at the time she was only six years old. Here at this time of my life I was faced with 3 beautiful daughters and living unhappy, unfilled and on the welfare system. It was a hard time after the birth of my twin girls. I started to get closer to God and my life was changing and I was feeling good again. Within a few months of going to church I became a member of Alie Church in St. Stephen SC and I gave my life to Christ in May of 1995. My mind needed a change and I was still making unwise decisions about money and not paying my bills. I was now faced with an evictions notice and was in need of $1000. God did bless me with the money from a person that had a genuine compassionate heart, but was still unhappy and not able to face myself combined with all the confusions of my family and having an ungrateful heart towards the one that helped me with the $1000. I moved within a few months and left a nice place when my twins were about 13 months old and moved to Georgia after God told me not to move and I gave it a year and moved in with my sister. The decision to move to College Park, Georgia was not my plan. I didn't consider all the things I would have loose and made a wrong decision out of negative emotions hurt by my family trying to control my life. Running away from problems was not the thing to do because problems only get worst. That is what happened to me and my three girls. The first few days was good, different because we had no privacy at all and all of a sudden my oldest daughter, Shadey took sick and had to be hospitalized for pneumonia. She was in a bad case and I didn't have insurance for her after just moving from South Carolina to College Park, Georgia and I was a nervous wreck with no money, no plan and guilt. At that time it was just a few days after my husband moved from NYC to GA and he had no money either and I had to call her dad from NYC to help me. While she stayed in the hospital he was there and we had to wear a mask every time we came in the room to see her to prevent her from coughing germs.

She became stronger, then her dad left to go back to NY. I enrolled her in school in Georgia. I was in a position to think about what my move was going to be. The plan was my husband was going to get a job and I was looking for work as well then he asked his boss to hire me. Our plan was we were both going to work and save money and find an apartment in College Park, Georgia for our family, but it didn't work out that way. I missed my cycle and was pregnant. My husband and my sister's boyfriend became good hanging buddies and they started to use crack-cocaine and was spending monies we didn't have, and before you knew it we was into a state of nothingness and confusion. So in that small one bedroom apartment where me and my husband slept on a mattress on the floor by the kitchen while my children slept on the couch. A few weeks ahead of us we were all headed for a big collision. So it did slowly, but surely I quit my job after I help get my fired from his job because I found out his lover moved to GA from NY with her now 3-months old baby. And stranger things started to happen. I was hitting rock bottom and didn't know how to stop it. It was too late to go back to the stable place I had before I moved to GA because I left things in a mess and I refused to move back home to my dad's house after making a mess of things. I allowed pride and fear to keep me paralyzed from going back to peace. So after everything started to crumble, after 2 months me being there, my story changed. My husband left and was now living with his lover and their brand new baby because she moved from NYC to Georgia and my sister's boyfriend was in and out using drugs and taking her through hell. We had our gas out we couldn't cook, we didn't have money to pay the gas bill, food was getting lower and lower, and I was not getting any help from my husband and here I was pregnant again and I made a mess of things and didn't know how I was going to care for my 3 girls and myself. So it was there in Atlanta that I applied for welfare again. I don't remember all the details, but I know it was a much longer process for whatever reasons. I was in a desperate state and was ashamed of myself for leaving my stable home to come to this place of hopelessness, but what kept me strong was God. I found a church while living with my sister and I started to feel a lot better. My circumstances didn't change right away, but I was gaining strength and wisdom. While I started to go more and more one evening in church I was sitting closer to the front and for some reason I looked back and there was the woman my husband left me for sitting behind me. Chills ran down my body and for a moment I just froze. Then a few minutes later she was gone so from that moment on I really did not feel good about going to that church with the thoughts and feelings that I was going to see her and I purpose to come just so I can see her and have words for her, but it never happen like that again. So still in a situation for a need for food, I made a phone call and explained my situation and was now given food stamps. Prior to the phone call my husband did come around occasionally with a little money or a bag or two of groceries and things changed in the area of not having food knowing my kids had little food. I sacrificed myself and the baby I was carrying scrapping of what was left, but it changed, but I was still faced with the fact that my husband and my sister's boyfriend used drugs with our rent monies and we were getting further and further behind and we had to move or get evicted, put out on the street with all our belongings. I didn't know what to do it was a short time I've moved to GA and now we were faced with a situation.

My oldest daughter's father had empathy for me and was going to help me get an apartment, but once he went down South to visit his family, he stopped over to see my dad and his story changed. He couldn't help me so I was faced with a decision to allow my oldest daughter to go back and live with her father until I get on my feet. That was a hard heartfelt decision and it hurt so deeply, but I thought about her well being. I was not in a position to give her a home because I was forced to go to a shelter. Here I was pregnant and I had these kids, my baby twins and I had to agree to allow my child to go back to Harlem NY and my husband is not helping me and it hurt.

Follow up with Volume 1 Contributors
Latashia R. Glover

It's been 8 years since my breakdown and well as you can tell that and many other situations which had followed did not kill me, but made me a heck of a lot stronger! I now stand on what I call the 4 P's of life, Power, Perseverance, Prayer and Persistence. I also had to do some self-evaluating, making sure that not only I was who I wanted to be, but also who GOD has ordained me to be. I continue to walk by faith and by doing so I've learned that through every lesson taught there is a test given and that test is actually an evaluation of the person you strive to be. Don't get me wrong I still make mistakes and things still happen good and bad in my life, but with God's help and my 4 P's, I seem to make it through. This is supposed to be my follow up story, but it's turning into my personal testimony and thanks is all that I can offer right now. Many doors have opened up for me because of this awesome book and I personally want to thank Kiwan for that! I am definitely continuing my journey and path towards Women's Empowerment and assisting Single Parents. I also have begun my career as a Motivational Speaker which also includes my own team of Empowerment Speakers (Thank You Jeeesusss!!) Lol. I'm currently in a healthy relationship that is definitely going to become apart of my future. Last, but not least I can finally say that I am no longer dependent on the Welfare System!! Because God gave me visions and has sent me angels (Kiwan) that keeps me motivated and consistently focused on challenging myself on a daily basis I will continuously pay my blessings forward and onward in order to help the next person who may be in need.

Shalonda 'Treasure' Williams

One of the things that I am most grateful for is the fact that God saw fit to give me the desire to change my mindset. It is one thing to be in poverty and a whole other thing to have a poverty mindset. There was a time when the latter was all me.

Not only did I live in housing, have food stamps, have medical assistance, have welfare assistance, but I thought I would always be in that place. I knew that another life existed, but I didn't necessarily believe that I could ever live it. I wanted more, but the life I had was comfortable. At least I was on my own and could come and go as I pleased without worrying what someone else thought. It was ok with me.

What I didn't realize was that it was only a place that I was passing through. The experience was what I needed in order for me to fully understand the people that I was destined to help. I was in a place where I was okay with settling for less just to get by. Dreaming was lame and living out your purpose was for the big time preachers and gurus. I was to go to school, get a "real" job and take care of my family… and that was that. Everything else could and should wait. The funny thing is that I always encouraged others to go after more and I was willing to settle. Go figure!

So, here is my big confession... TODAY I AM FREE FROM THE NONSENSE!!! ☺ I am free to see clearly and to go after a lifestyle that doesn't tell me that I am only worth the minimum. See, I understand now that it's okay to accept help when necessary, but it is not okay, for me, to stay in that place. It was so much of a comfortable lifestyle that most of us spent more time making sure that we stayed within the eligibility requirements. We stunted our own growth... ON PURPOSE! But, I am grateful for new insight.

Welfare was a resource and still is at times, but it was not meant to be comfortable. So, now that I am free to see clearly, I vow to help others see clear as well. I had always been a giver anyway, so now I walk in my rightful place.

First: Never allow anyone else to define you or what you are worth. It is okay to dream big and to know that you can one day live that dream. – I have always been creative. I used to dream of being an actress or a singer. What happened to those dreams? Well, I allowed others to tell me what I was worth and what I had to go after. The only way that I would be able to make it is if I finished school. That was my only ticket to being successful. Now I know that there is so much more to life and I am not ashamed to pursue it!

Second: You are worth more than nickels and dimes. You don't have to stand in line for the rest of your life, waiting for someone to throw you a scrap to eat. – I knew people back in the day who knew that dates for every organization that was offering a check, food or vouchers. I wasn't that good, but I knew of a few. It became the norm and that wasn't acceptable.

Third: Always be a giver and not just a taker. Taking leads to an endless cycle of lack. – Deep within myself I have always been a giver. I used to stand in some of those lines looking at other people with pity in my heart. I used to pray that God would bless them to be in a better place. I used to give my socks and hair bows away as a child. I used to share my lunch with the "poor" kids at school. I did all this without realizing that I was just as "poor." I was standing in that same line for help. My mother was struggling to get me those socks. I was also on reduced or free lunch in school. What I now know is that the real reason that I could never get completely comfortable on welfare was because I was not designed to only take… I was created to be a giver. Being a giver makes room for you to prosper. Being a taker only leaves room for you to need to take again and again; never having enough of your own.

Fourth: Throw away the poverty mindset. Thinking "poor" will keep you poor. Enough said. Go back to your dreams and plan to fulfill them. If the big names can do it, so can I; so can you. You no longer have to be stunted.

I thank welfare for being there when I needed it, but I thank God for changing my mindset and setting me on course for more!

Strong Woman by Tina Alexis

Wow! Look at you!
Enduring all of the pains, hurts and
disappointments that this life can bring.
Yet you Still forge ahead and do what
you gotta do for your precious offspring
God Chose you for this most challenge of not only
making something out of nothing,
But making enough of it so that
It will last!
I know that you may often feel that no one
truly understands or feels your pain
But they do because there are a million more just like you!
Strong, beautiful soldiers who have this
most tired some cross to bare-
So don't ever for one second, make yourself
believe that no one cares because
I do, your children do and most importantly
GOD does TOO!
You see GOD designed you that way.
To strengthen you and wipe your tears away.
So that those beautiful eyes of your can see the beauty and promise
of a New   Day!
You are beautiful Blessed!

ABOUT TO FLY

As a child I stand in the middle of the field
surround with mother nature beautiful green grass
with my arms spread out like an eagle with wings
as my head is slightly tilted back as my eyes gaze into the sky
Thinking there are times that some people might try to clip my
wings but it is almost Spring.
There are time the very people you believed in will throw stones at
you and attempt to cloud and trouble your spirit
There are many times cruel words are spoken but as a woman of
God with a heart of an angel; the innocent of a child my spirit rush
back into me and said it is time to soar now stretch out your arms
like an eagle as you lean back trust God and know that God
got this and the next one after that Yes I will always believe
that something mighty wonderful is about to happen
Is my claim today
Strong enough to not shed another tear drop
closing my ears to all negativity
it time to do some spring cleaning in my life
so people can't hurt me anymore
with their sharp tongue like a knife
while God will control this map
I know I will fly
over, and over again my spirit

will not die for its time for me to fly.

Oh yes, I do believe something mighty, mighty wonderful is about to happen for me.

Copyright 2012
Luella Hill-Dudley
Antioch, CA
luelladudley@sbcglobal.net
www.luellaspeak.com

Contributor Information and Family Resources

Kiwan N. Fitch, Author
The EmPOWERment Corp., LLC
Columbia, SC
www.kiwanfitch.com
www.confessionsofawelfaremom.com
Kiwanfitch@gmail.com

Stacy Rodgers, MSW, ACSW, DVS, WTS
PURE I.M.A.G.E.S., Inc.
Jersey City, New Jersey
pureimagesinc@yahoo.com

Lisa Dixon
New York
brnxlisa9@yahoo.com

Tina Alexis
Author of "Life Is Simply About Living".
New Jersey
www.tinaalexis.com

Terri Clay, Inspirational Speaker
CEO and Founder of Terri Clay Enterprises
Atlanta, Georgia
www.terriclayinspires.com
www.steppinoutofthebox.org

LaTersa Blakely
Cleveland, Ohio
lblakely2010@gmail.com
www.LaTersaBlakely.com

Stephanie Wilson
What's Really Cooking? Advice from the Stove Top to the Table
Catering Service and Spices
Bayonne, NJ
SRWilson2508@yahoo.com
www.whatsreallycooking.com

Regina Lewis
Editor in Chief, The Work from Home Digest
Akron, Ohio
www.theworkfromhomeclassroom.com
theworkfromhomeclassroom@gmail.com

Dana Neal
Milwaukee, Wisconsin
Coach Dana Enterprises
www.coachdana.biz

Iniece Payton
Jersey City, NJ
IniecePayton@gmail.com

Britney Torres
New Jersey

Christina Stankiewickz
New Jersey

Charlsey Sheppard, Founder
Creating Confidence LLC.
Atlanta, Georgia
www.CreatingConfidenceNetwork.com

Joe Cherey
Wild Heart Social Media
Topeka, Kansas
j3cheray@gmail.com

Sherry Blair
ISIS Innovative Specialists Inspirational Services, LLC
Montclair, NJ
info@isisnj.us

Angela Fitch
Freedom from Frenzy Computer Services
Jersey City, NJ
angela.fitch@gmail.com

Latashia Glover
DDCT Enterprises Inc; Single Parents United Corp
GOLD Expectations Employment and Resource Center LL
Euclid, OH
LatashiaGlover@yahoo.com

Shalonda "Coach Treasure" Williams
Love Walk Motivational Services
Savannah, GA

Barbara E. Milton II. PhD, LCSW
CEO of Social Work Practice for Resilience, LLC
North Bergen, NJ
DrMiltonLCSW@gmail.com

Bibliography of Resources

(http://socialwork.wayne.edu/syllabi/sw_5755.pdf)

by **Dr. Barbara Milton**

Policy, Poverty, Social Justice, Welfare Reform

The Administrative for Children and Families (ACF), within the Department of Health and Human Services (HHS) is responsible for federal programs which promote the economic and social well-being of families, children, and communities. The web site has press releases, organizational information, fact sheet on ACF programs, and links to other, related sites of the federal government. Programs described at this web site include: welfare, foster care adoption, family preservation, child protection, Head Start, childcare, child support enforcement, services to youth, programs to strengthen communities, and special programs to such populations as the developmentally disabled, refugees, and Native Americans. www.acf.dhhs.gov

Bureau of the Census has a web site on sources of data on children and on children's programs such as child care and child support enforcement. It lists current reports on children produced by the Census Bureau and give links to census demographic data at the federal and local levels. Is also gives links to other federal sources of data on children, such as the National Center for Health Statistics. www.census.gov/populations/www/socdemo/children

Child Trends, Inc. Child Trends, Inc. is a nonprofit organization dedicated to research focused on children, youth, and families. The web site offers comprehensive data on how welfare reform affects children. www.childtrends.org

Child Welfare League of America is the Nation's oldest and largest membership-based child welfare organization. It is and association of almost 1,000 public and private nonprofit child welfare agencies. The website lists and services offered to members and also provide advocacy information concerning current policy proposals of the federal government. www.cwla.org

Children's Defense Fund is an advocacy organization for children in America who cannot vote, lobby, or speak for themselves. It pays particular attention to the needs of poor minority children and those with disabilities. The web site offers current information on federal policy initiatives, and encourages citizen involvement in the policy process. www.childrendefense.org

Handsnet is a web site offering information, training and technical assistance to nonprofit agencies, using the resources of the world wide web. It provides bulletins and summaries of recent federal policy initiatives of interest to the human service community. www.handsnet.org

Institute for Women Policy Research The institute was established to research policies that impact women. A portion of the web site is committed to welfare reform and contains information on domestic violence, reproduction, education, and issues that impact women in relation to welfare reform. The site also has a welfare monitoring list serve which provides an online forum for interested individuals to discuss welfare reform. www.iwpr.org

KIDS COUNT, project of an Annie E. Casey Foundation, is a national and state-by-state effort to track the status of children in the United States. By providing policymakers and citizens with benchmarks of child well-being, KIDS COUNT seek to secure better futures for all children. The annual KIDS COUNT Data Book uses the best available data to measure the educational, social, economic, and physical well-being of children. The website provides the information from the KIDS COUNT reports. www.aecf.org/aeckids.htm

The National Center for Children in Poverty, The NCCP promotes policies and programs that work to reduce child poverty. The web site provides statistics about children along with information on how welfare reform affects children. www.cpmcnet.columbia.edu/dept/nccp/

The Urban Institute: Assessing the New Federalism. The Urban Institute provides extensive information on social and economic issues. Assessing the Federalism is the Urban Institute's project examining welfare reform. In addition to information about all aspects of welfare reform, the site offer thorough and extensive research related specifically to families and children. The web site also has a database with information about the efforts of each state in addressing welfare reform. www.federalism.urban.org

Welfare Information Network is a foundation funded project to help states and communities obtain the information, policy analysis, and technical assistance they need to develop and implement welfare reforms. It has a clearinghouse of welfare reform related information, including special web sites on teenage parenting, child support, and all aspects of child welfare. The site includes summaries of federal legislation concerning families and children and a calendar of welfare related events. It provides links to related organizations, policy analysis research centers, state agencies, and technical assistance resources, including "best practices" projects www.welfareinfo.org.
The site devoted specifically to child welfare issues is: www.welfareinfor.org/childwelf

Family Support and Prevention Sites

Family Education Network. An educationally focused web site for parents, with resources, an on-lien community, and links to other sites. Education partners include the PTA and the National Association of School Administrators. www.familyeducation.com

Family Resource Coalition. The Family Resource Coalition is an information and support organization for a wide range of family support programs. The web site describes the organization and provides links to state initiatives in family support. www.pavin.com/clients/frc/frcn

Family Resource Information, Education, and Network Development Service. This organization offers a range of services designed to assist states, tribal organizations, and local programs in the development of community-based family resource programs and networks. www.frca.org/ntap2

Father & Family Link. Produced by the National Center of Fathers and Families at the University of Pennsylvania, this comprehensive web site provides current, reliable information on research, practice, policy and programs related to father in families.
www.ncoff.gse.upenn.edu/fatherlink/index

National Parent Information Network. This web site offers resources from ERIC Clearinghouse and Elementary and Early Childhood Education and the ERIC Clearinghouse on Urban Education, provides information to parents and those who work with parents, and fosters the exchange of parenting materials. Includes information for urban/minority families. www.npin.org

National Campaign to Prevent Teen Pregnancy. This national advocacy organization works to prevent teen pregnancy by supporting values and stimulating actions that are consistent with a pregnancy-free adolescence. The web site includes information for parents, teenagers, advocates, and scholars. www.teenpregnancy.org

National Center for Missing and Exploited Children. This organization spearheads national efforts to locate and recover missing children and raises public awareness about ways to prevent child abduction, molestation, and sexual exploitation. Established in 1984, NCMEC operates under a Congressional mandate and works in conjunction with the U.S. Department of Justice's Office of Juvenile Justice and Delinquency Prevention. The web site contains educational materials to prevent abduction. www.missingkids.org

National Indian Child Welfare Association. This organization serves tribes in the United States and helps them enhance their capacity to deliver quality child welfare services. The site contains information on community development, public policy, and information exchange. www.nicwa.org

NativeWeb. This is the web site of a collective project to provide a cyber-community for Earth's indigenous peoples, with an extensive search capacity and links to other sites. www.nativeweb.org

Parents' Place. A web site run by and for parents, it contains parenting information on a wide range of subjects, shopping information, and extensive search facility, and numerous chat rooms. www.parentsplace.com

Welfare Information Network: Teen Parents. The Welfare Information Network offers up-to-date policy information on issues relating to public welfare. A special section of their web site in devoted to policies concerning teen pregnancy. www.welfareinfo.org/teen

National Resource for Family Centered Practice. This federally funded resources center which provides technical assistance and training to states and programs, has a comprehensive web site which includes lists of material available, bibliographies, and *The Prevention Report.* www.uiowa.edu/~nrcfcp

National Family Preservation Network. The central coordinating point for a network of family preservation staff and programs. www.nfpn.org

Day Care and Child Development

Families and Work Institute. The Families and Work Institute is a non-profit organization that addresses the changing nature of work and family life. It is committed to finding research-based strategies that foster mutually supportive connections among workplaces, families, and communities. The web site describes the institute's research on a broad range of issues on the connection between work and family life, with extensive links to other sites. www.familiesandwork.org

National Child Care Information Center. The Center is pare of the Children's Bureau, U.S. Department of Health and Human Services. It disseminates child care information in response to requests from States, Territories and Tribes, policymakers, parents, programs, organizations, providers and the public. The Center also publishes the Child Care Bulletin six times a year. www.nccic.org

National Institute of Child Health and Human Development. The NICHD administers a multidisciplinary program of research, research training, and public information, nationally and within its own facilities, on prenatal development as well as maternal, child and family health. The web site offers access to NICHD publications. www.nih.gov/nichd

National Network for Child Care. This non-profit, education organization affiliated with the Cooperative Extension programs of state universities attempts to increase and strengthen the quality of non-parental care environments using the expertise of Cooperative Extension's nationwide dissemination system. It offers an e-mail listserv for communication on day care, support and assistance to day care providers and users, and a newsletter. The web site is an internet source of over 1000 publications and resources relate to child care. www.exnet.iastate.edu/Pages/families/nncc/homepage

Working Mother Lifenet. This web site provides information on day care for working parents, with results of state surveys on licensing laws and other consumer information.
www.womweb.com

Child Neglect and Abuse

American Humane Association. This national advocacy organization for abused and neglected children has numerous resources on policy and practice in child preventive services. www.americanhumane.org

National Clearinghouse on Child Abuse and Neglect Information. This is a national resource for professionals seeking information of prevention, identification, and treatment of child abuse and neglect, related child welfare issues. The National Center for Child Abuse and Neglect is accessed at this web site. It contains numerous resources and links to other sites. www.calib.com/nccanch

National Committee to Prevent Child Abuse. The web site of a national advocacy organization whose purpose is to prevent and reduce child maltreatment. The site has numerous resources for advocates, including information packets, publications of statistics and trends, and lists of local chapters. www.childabuse.org

Children's Bureau. Administration for Children, Youth, and Families, U.S. Department of Health and Human Services. Contains information on federal initiatives in foster care and

adoption and statistics, child abuse and neglect, and other programs.
www.acf.dhhs.gov/programs/cb

Foster Care and Adoption

Children's Bureau. Administration for Children, Youth, and Families, Department of Health and Human Services. AFCARS (the Adoption and Foster Care Analysis and Reporting System). This government site provides data on foster care.
www.acf.dhha.gov/programs/cb/stats/afcars

Child Welfare League of America. This organization has a general child welfare site, with specific pages related to developments in foster care, and lists of topically related publications provided by CWLA. www.cwla.org

National Foster Parent Association. Information on becoming a foster parent is available at this site. This site explains the purpose of the National Foster Parent Association and provides membership information. It offers a comprehensive site called KidSource which addresses information on children, newborn through adolescence, as it relates to fostering.
www.kidsource.com/nfpa/index

National Resource Center for Permanency Planning. Provides information services, training and technical assistance to ensure that children have safe families to grow up in. This site focuses on the following issues: Permanency planning, kinship foster care, concurrent planning, family group decision making and HIV/AIDS.
www.hunter.cuny.edu/socwork

The Evan P. Donaldson Adoption Institute. Provides up-to-date information on research, policy and practice in adoption. www.adoptioninstitute.org [June, 1998]

National Adoption Information Clearinghouse. Established by the U.S. Congress to provide information on all aspects of adoptions, including infant and intercountry adoption and adopting children with special needs. www.calib.com/naic [June, 1998]

Juvenile Court and Legal Issues
The following sites provide copies of statutes, case decisions, analyses and commentary on legal issues affecting children in the juvenile and family court system. All sites begin with http://www. unless indicated other wise.

Center for Children & the Law - abanet.org/child/home
Center for Law & Social Policy - epn.org/clasp

Code of Federal Regulations - access.gpo.gov/nara/cfr/cfr-table-search

Cornell Legal Information Institute - (no www) supct.law.conell.edu/law.cornell.edu

National Council of Juvenile & Family Court Judges – ncjfcj.unr.edu

The Juvenile Justice Clearinghouse – fsu.edu/~crimdo/jjclearinghouse/jjcleringhouse

Thomas - US Congress - (no www) thomas.loc.gov

The United States Supreme Court - uscourts.gov

Department of Health and Human Services - os.dhhs.gov

Office of Juvenile Justice and Delinquency Prevention – ojjdp.dhhs.gov

www.ingramcontent.com/pod-product-compliance
Lightning Source LLC
Chambersburg PA
CBHW052057070526
44584CB00017B/2228

What Pastors Don't Tell You About The Prosperity Message

...Uncovering the reasons wealth stays in the pulpit and seldom reaches the pews!

Leah Pride

Published
2021

WHAT PASTORS DON'T TEACH YOU ABOUT THE PROSPERITY MESSAGE

© 2021 by Leah Pride

All rights reserved.

No portion of this book may be reproduced, stored in a retrieval system, or transmitted in any form or by means—electronic, mechanical, photocopy, recording, scanning, or other excerpt for brief quotations in critical reviews or articles, without prior written permission of the publisher.

ISBN# 978-1-4507-5641-9

Edited by Beverly Connelly and Dawn Jenkins

Published in Houston, Texas, by
This Rock Entertainment, LLC

Scripture quotation used from King James Version (KJV)

www.LeahPride.com

www.This-Rock.com

Printed in the United States of America